rayer repares

the

ay

Pastor Darlinda Turner

(Contributor) Rev. Reuben T. Jones, Jr.

Pastor Darlinda Turner & Bishop R.T. Jones, Jr.

Hollis Media Group
Publisher

Copyright page

ISBN 9798486236259

All scripture quotations are taken from the King James Version, American Standard Version, and New Living Translation of the Bible

Publisher: Hollis Media Group

Copyright year: 2021

CONTENTS

Dedication

My mission is to inspire and encourage the saints to go back to their first love, Prayer.

In addition, it is my sincere desire to reach the masses and share effective tools to train, fortify, and help identify grey areas that negate from living one's best life and renew their zeal for God's plan.

Introduction

This book can be used as an instrumental resource in helping you identify the need for Prayer as an essential lifestyle choice. The tools/prayers we shared are transformative; prayers that will empower you to live consistently and how to pray about everything.

What we teach?

How to pray.
Why you should pray.

The power of prayer.

How to organize life for prayer; and what prayer principles are to name a few.

Just as Christ Jesus prayed for you and I, we must also spend time praying for others. (John 17).

During this Pandemic we have all increased our prayer life; our homes became a safe haven (spiritual sanctuary) even for some who left serving in the church. The scare of the unknown was an effective catalyst for ALL to get before God and renew our hearts and commitment.

I, like countless others had to increase my prayer life exponentially as the burdens of the *unknown and loss of life* became insurmountable in the news, and in the body of Christ.

Several takeaways in this book will help you remove barriers to your faith walk and show you how to conquer stagnation, remove limitation, doubt, and all other spiritual obstacles confronting you.

Without question, it is more evident the present tone in the world calls for us to develop a prayer life. Make no mistake, having one was always required but now the necessity is dire.

The spiritual warfare is constantly expanding; the overreach into the affairs of humanity by the devil has reached every facet of life.

Our babies are aborted in the womb, our toddlers are brainwashed to believe they can change their identity. Teenagers, opting for gender surgery, moms and dads in many families are noncommittal, and the laws of the land run afoul to God.

This dispensation demands of us to get resolution quicker, to cast off idleness and go after the spoken promise with vigor and tenacity.

The target is your family and everything God promised you. The satanic invasion of weights/wicked oppression of darkness are designed to bomb your runway; to prevent you from rising and setting others free with your ascent. We show you how to fight back, how to climb higher consistently, and create an oasis for you with God.

Also, what is discussed is what prayer is. This will simplify the process and help you get a grasp of what's in your hand and how to deploy the power of God through prayer to change your life.

Prayer is a *language* that has been spoken in every generation, culture and the world.

Prayer infuses the spirit with strength, illuminates and penetrates *darkness* throughout the world. My personal experience with having a prayer-life is it's my lifeline to God. Without communicating with God, I would be lost.

We encourage you to pray because when you do God's ears are always open. Your voice is like music to His ears. When you ask and *petition* God to answer your prayers, it is a welcome invitation He extends to everyone.

CHAPTER 1

PRAYER?

Prayer is a petition (a request). It is an evolving avenue of interacting with God. Prayer is communication with God. Prayer is done by those who trust the power of the word and thought. Jesus taught the people to say the Lord's prayer. Matthew 6:9-13. Prayer can be spoken, silent (no talking), or in a song. It can be used to praise God or to ask for something including help and forgiveness.

Our responsibility ...

We are commanded to pray. Even though God knows our needs before we even think to ask Him. We can trust that God, in His providence will meet our needs – yet still we are commanded to pray. We do not pray in order to make sure God knows, or to remind him, or to give Him a nudge. We pray to acknowledge our *complete* dependence upon the Lord, this glorifies Him, and is a requirement.

Prayer has to do with our entire being. It takes over our body, mind, and soul when we pray. *Prayer* affects the *whole person.* Your *total being* must be given to God when you pray.

Prayer is an opportunity to spend time with God, and to learn and understand the heart of the *Creator.*

In John 15:15, Jesus says, "He no longer calls us his servants, but calls us his friends". Talking with God develops a deeper relationship with Him. Jesus taught, "When you pray, do not be like the hypocrites, for they love to pray standing in the synagogues and on the street corners to be seen by men. But when you pray, go into your room, close the door and pray to your father who is unseen, and He will reward you openly".

Prayer can be both Private and Corporate. (Matthew 6:5-8) Jesus said that prayer should be a private time between God and the worshipper. Jesus does not mean that it is wrong to pray with others, but *when we pray with others,* prayers should be sincere and for the right motives.

The more we pray the world will be better and mightier against the forces of evil, and wickedness will cease *to dominate the atmosphere.* We must understand that Prayer isn't a one phase operation; it is a *decontaminator* and a preemptive tool to apply to all situations. Prayer will purify the air; it will destroy the contagion of all evil. Prayer is not fitful, or a short-lived *practice . . . it is a lifestyle.*

Prayer is a voice that goes into God's ears, and when you pray according to God's will your prayer is always heard and will be answered. Your prayers live as long as God's ears are open to holy pleas, as God's heart is alive to holy things.

Prayer has shaped this world over centuries, and prayers are *eternal.* When we die our prayers will always live before God, and His heart is set on them. Our prayers will always outlive us for generations and generations to come. Prayer will outlive this world. Prayer will strengthen the incoming generations, just like the prayers our forefathers did for us. So, don't give up and never stop praying.

I remember as a little girl the saints singing *"don't stop praying, the Lord is nigh. Don't stop praying He'll hear your cry. The Lord has promised, and His word is true. Don't stop praying, He'll answer you."*

I can still hear the prayers of the saints in my life. While we are here in this world, we must store up prayers. *It's akin to placing them* in the storehouse of heaven so when we need them, we can call up to heaven and ask God to release them to target any situation.

Your prayers are not placed in the iCloud, Facebook, Instagram, Zoom, Twitter, or in a book on the shelf. When you call on the name of Jesus at any time, answers will come. You don't have to wait to get a "LIKE", or see how many people looked at your request or worry about who has the highest number of "Followers" to make some money and go live on social media. My God is greater than all you can imagine because He created all of it. "God is the Author and the Finisher of our faith," and no man can be God. You must hold on to the Horns of the Altar – don't give up and never stop praying.

Prayer is like the capital stock in heaven which Christ invested in as the father's work is being achieved upon the earth. You must know that your prayer allows God to cause change in the earth; it will revolutionize, cause angels to move powerfully, and expeditiously.

God's blueprint is shaped as our prayers are more numerous, more efficient. And prayer puts God in operation full force in the world . . .

He intervenes when we invite him through supplication.

Prayer is the principal application that keeps us sanctified (set apart). We must let prayer be the key or principal thing in the morning and the bolt at night. When you go down on your knees that is the best fight against sin.

Lifestyle . . .

Daniel knelt upon his knees three times a day in prayer. Solomon got down on his knees in prayer at the dedication of the temple. Our Lord in Gethsemane prostrated himself in that memorable season of praying just before his betrayal. You must learn to have a praying spirit and be consistent in order to get great results. You will win more battles on your knees than sparring in the flesh... Some situations you will only resolve through prayer.

The prayer of faith is the only power in the whole universe and the greatest power that man cannot trace with a philosophical conclusion. Prayer can go where no man has gone before and is the conduit to using applied faith (action) to overcome.

Prayer is the established principle and path to experiencing the move of the Spirit in the Kingdom. It tells us in Matthew 7:7: You must learn that prayer is the secret to success in Christ's kingdom. When you pray you move from false premises to God's promises.

My pastor, Bishop Jones used to say, *"Preaching moves man, prayer moves God. More things are wrought through prayer than the world has ever dreamed possible."*

CHAPTER 2

I KNOW WHAT PRAYER CAN DO

When you look at the world today, it seems as though we have lost our minds, principles, morals, and sadly the Church is losing its love for the things of God. The distractions infused by access to personalities, technology, and other frivolous systems are killing off the saints.

Designed to kill, steal, and destroy...

We must realize the world's system is designed to eliminate the presence of God; it's a system that is set up for the believers to fail. It starts in the mind and trickles down and controls our entire being. You have questions about the very thing that has come upon us. Sickness, hatred, stress, depression, oppression, strife, backbiting, hunger, murder, lying, and spiritual wickedness. These are the things that God prepared us to conquer and warned against in the Bible that will come, and people still won't believe.

Since March 2020, we have seen the handiwork of God in this Pandemic, COVID-19. We must remain steadfast and unmovable in this spiritual walk with God. God is looking at the saints and holding us all accountable for the work assigned to us. We must believe that prayer will help us to stay focused and on track. Unequivocally, I can speak to and about the power of my witness regarding prayer. I lived through some of the darkest days of my life battling cancer, but I made it. I prayed.

The Saints prayed for me that I would be healed. I know what prayer can do because I am still here. Prayer will always change the world's system. Man will always line up to God's word because he is made in the image of Him.

Another time in my life when I thought that I wasn't going to make it, happened in 2008. I had been living in Delaware for two years. I had four children and my husbandworked. This day he was going into work late. He received a call that one of his clients was rushed to the hospital. He was out riding his bike, so he had to go in because he was the supervisor. He seemed ok when he left.

It was around 2-3 hours later as he was sitting in his car waiting for staff, he had a heart attack, right in front of the hospital. When he was released, I said Lord, please keep him covered under the blood. It was on a Sunday that he preached at this church and said, "When you don't know what to do about pain in your chest, just lay the Bible on it". Not knowing that prayer was preparing the way for him. Being in front of the

19

hospital saved his life and he is now a living testimony. I pray for my husband every night while he is sleeping, asking God to protecthim from danger seen and unseen. As women and men of God we must be in position day and night. Warriors must always stay on the battlefield.

My ministry *"Women on the Battlefield"* has been in existence since 2006, it started with four women on the phone constantly in prayer for the souls of others. This ministry is dedicated to praying, interceding, and staying in the War room of prayer. Over the years we learned that God needs us as warriors to stand and fight for those women whoare lost, discouraged, broken, used and abused by the ones who said they love them.

This ministry has reached people all over the world. We are still on the prayer line everyMonday night at 8:30 pm. We have dedicated ourselves to remain on our knees for the people. Continue to be dedicated whatever God has assigned your hands to do!

I have seen so many healed and delivered. Being persistent in prayer will reach the heart of God. Ask the woman who was persistent when she kept going to the *unjust* judge. The Parable of the Unjust Judge (also known as the Parable of the Importunate Widowor the Parable of the Persistent Widow), is one of the parables of Jesus which appears in the Gospel of Luke (Luke 18:1–8). In it, a judge who lacks compassion is repeatedly approached by a poor widow, seeking justice.

CHAPTER 3

PRAYER POEM

Prayer Poem

(I know what prayer can do)

Prayer is essential to our life

Prayer is the lifeline of my blood stream

Prayer allows you to connect to the throne of grace

Prayer will allow you to be in the presence of the Lord at any time of the day

Prayer is like your breath of fresh air

Prayer puts you in the place of peace and serenity

Prayer will give you hope

Prayer will heal you inside and outside

Prayer causes you to want God more and more

Prayer will cause you to close out everything around you to get in the presence of God

Prayer will give you strength like no other

Prayer will teach how to trust Him

Prayer takes you in the presence of God so you will hear His voice for your life and direction

Prayer is the key to unlock all the areas of your life that you close the doors on

Prayer will tell you how to live and breathe

Prayer is the only language to heaven

Prayer changes your language

Prayer gives you the ability to move freely

Chapter 4

PRAY WITH YOUR
WHOLE HEART

When you pray you must have faith that all your Prayers are answered. In the natural you might not see it but after all that I've been through I just know that it's coming to pass. Your prayers will be answered when you believe. You must tell your situation to God because God knows what you are going through. He is your Keeper if you want to be kept.

Prayer is like the heartbeat that carries all our veins through our body.

"Blessed are they that keep his testimonies, and that seek him with the whole heart." Psalms 119:2 KJV

The "HEART"

The Bible uses the word "heart" primarily to refer to the ruling center of the whole person, the spring of all desires. According to the Bible, the heart is the center not only of spiritual activity, but of all the operations of human life. "Heart" and "soul" are often used interchangeably.

What is the connection between
the heart and mind?

The two organs communicate via the muscular walls around the heart, which are connected to the brain in the circulatory system. As the brain releases hormones telling the body what to do, receptor cells in your blood vessels pick up these messages.

The brain gets to take a little break here because the heart will actually beat all by itself. In addition to the intrinsic heartbeat that the heart has all by itself, the autonomic nervous system is a separate part of the brain and the brain function that can either speed up or slow down your heart.

Why the heart is so powerful when you pray?

The word heart appears over one thousand times in the Bible making it the most common anthropological term in Scripture. It denotes a person's center for both physical and emotional-intellectual-moral activities; sometimes it is used figuratively for any inaccessible thing.

.

The heart is the center of physical activity. "Heart" denotes to both ancient and modern peoples the beating chest organ protected by the rib cage. Ancient people, however, understood the heart's physical function differently than in modern times. From their view point the heart was the central organ that moved the rest of the body. Ancients ate to strengthen the heart and so revive the body.

Abraham offers his weary guests food so that they might "sustain their hearts" and then go on their way (Gen 18:5).

You must understand that we need our heart strong so God can speak to us in prayer.

The heart as the Center of Hidden Emotional-Intellectual-Moral Activity. "Man looks at the outward appearance," says Samuel, "but the lord looks at the heart". (1 Sam 16:7).

The king's heart is unsearchable to humankind (Prov 25:3), but the Lord searches all hearts to reward all according to their conduct (Jer. 17:10). In the time of judgment God will expose the hidden counsels of the heart (1 Cor 4:5).

Jesus says that the heart's secrets are betrayed by the mouth, even as a tree's fruit discloses its nature. (Matt 12:33-34)

"A wise man's heart guides his mouth," says Solomon. (Prov 16:23). Most important, the mouth confesses what the heart trusts (Rom 10:9; cf. Deut 30:14).

When you pray you must seek God with your whole heart. Your heart is tender, and God created you to give it back to Him. God is looking for warriors that will pray with all their heart, mind and soul.

"In one word, the entire man without reservation must love God. So, it takes the same entire man to do the praying which God requires of men. All the powers of man must be engaged in it. God cannot tolerate a divided heart in the love He requires of men, neither can He bear with a divided man in praying. It requires the whole person to pray, praying is no easy task. Praying is far more than simply bending the knee and saying a few words by rote." (E.M. Bounds)

Jesus demonstrates while he was in the garden of Gethsemane that you must give up something to be in the presence of the Lord. Jesus engaged His whole heart when praying. When Jesus was praying it took His entire *will* to pray. We must become like Jesus when we pray and never give up. We must press until we get an answer.

The greatest commandment according to Jesus is, "Love the Lord your God with all your heart" (Matt 22:37). Love here is more than an emotion; it is a conscious commitment to the Lord.

Luke 22:40-44 (KJV)

"And when he was at the place, he said unto them, Pray that ye enter not into temptation. And he was withdrawn from them about a stone's cast, and knelt down, and prayed, Saying, Father, if thou be willing, remove this cup from me: nevertheless, not my will, but thine, be done. And being in agony he prayed more earnestly: and his sweat was as it were great drops of blood falling down to the ground."

Of course, God requires us to have a clean heart before him, however, His grace accepts the sinner as he is to start the transformation process... Through the word and application thereof God cleanses your heart. This is vitally important because a contaminated heart will block your prayers. And as you develop a committed prayer life your life will change because of the power of prayer.

Remember, "As water reflects the face, so one's life reflects the heart." The Good News: Your life is a reflection of the ideals and faith you hold in your heart.

The areas where you spend time and energy reveals what's really important to you. "Whoever pursues righteousness and love finds life, prosperity, and honor." This is FAVOR!

Chapter 5

PRAYERS TO GOD

We must reverence God in our prayers. These three powerful words are how we should come to the Throne of Grace: In Prayer, with Praise, and Thanksgiving

O Come, let us sing for joy to the Lord; Let us shout joyfully to the rock of our salvation. Let us come into his presence with thanksgiving; let us make a joyful noise to him with songs of praise! For the Lord is a great God, and a great King above all gods." Ps. 95:1-3

GIVE YOUR HEART TO GOD

Pray this prayer to God with a sincere heart. I SURRENDER MY LIFE TO YOU AND I BELIEVE THAT YOUR SON JESUS DIED ON THE CROSS FOR ME. I REPENT!!

Lord, teach me to offer you a heart of thanksgiving and praise in all my daily experiences of life. Teach me to be joyful always, to pray continually and to give thanks in all my circumstances. I accept them as Your will for my life (1 Thessalonians 5:16-18). Write down your date and time you gave your life over to Christ!

CHAPTER 6

LORD TEACH ME TO PRAY

In Scripture it reads: "And it came to pass, that, as he was praying in a certain place, when he ceased, one of his disciples said unto him, Lord, teach us to pray, as John also taught his disciples. And he said unto them, "When ye pray, say, Our Father which art in heaven, Hallowed be thy name. Thy kingdom come. Thy will be done, as in heaven, so on earth. Give us day by day our daily bread. And forgive us our sins; for we also forgive every one that is indebted to us. And lead us not into temptation; but deliver us from evil." Luke 11:1-4 KJV

When you ask God to teach you how to pray, He may place you in overwhelmed situations where we recognize that we have no choice but to pray! So, if you dare, you can with fear and trembling say, "Lord teach me to pray." It was after watching Jesus pray that a disciple was prompted to request instruction in praying. The Lord Jesus prayed often; it was a lifestyle so this should be an indicator to us that we must also pray often. We must model the life of Christ and total dependence on the Father.

Then Jesus prayed in the garden of Gethsemane; His prayer life and instructions on prayer are foundational as we struggle to grow in our prayer life. So many struggle to have or keep a prayer life. If you are struggling with your prayer life, you ought to then ask God to help you to follow the Lord's instruction so you can build your prayer life.

The disciples sitting at Jesus' feet implies that they were listening and communing with Him in prayer. So many of us are too busy to stop and listen to His instructions for our life, and if you had stopped to listen you probably would be farther along in life and in your spiritual walk with Christ. It's never too late to learn how to pray or reactivate your prayer life.

Start right now! God wants to hear your voice! Have faith to believe that he will hear your cry. "Give your life over to Him." God is here to make you whole again and when you communicate with Him through prayer, change comes. "Prayer still works."

In times past, you can say in Luke 11:1-4, should be called the disciples' prayer, since Jesus never needed to pray for forgiveness. The Lord gave this same model prayer on the Mount (Matt. 6:9-13). These prayer models are tools that should cause you to want to pray, and when we pray, we should focus on the Father's purpose and we should focus on the family's needs. Continue to ask the lord "Teach Me to Pray"

YOUR PRAYER HAS POWER

"Are any of you suffering hardships? You should pray. Are any of you happy? You should sing praises. Are any of you sick? You should call for the elders of the church to come and pray over you, anointing you with oil in the name of the Lord. Such a prayer offered in faith will heal the sick, and the Lord will make you well. And if you have committed any sins, you will be forgiven. Confess your sins to each other and pray for each other so that you may be healed. The earnest prayer of a righteous person has great power and produces wonderful results. The Old Testament prophet Elijah was as human as we are, and yet when he prayed earnestly that no rain would fall, none fell for three and a half years! Then, when he prayed again, the sky sent down rain and the earth began to yield its crops."

James 5:13-18 NLT Prayer can change and control the weather, other elements and YOU too!

CHAPTER 7

GOD IS CHANGING YOUR STORY

How many of you have a story you can tell; Or remember those shared? Can you remember how a story was told to you or about you? We all have a story to tell someone and it may take some of you the rest of your life to tell it. Remember your life is your story and your eulogy. Life for some has been a roller coaster that never stops, a sailboat with no sails, an airplane in turbulence, and seemingly a life incased in quicksand. We all can relate to some form of trouble in life. We have made some trouble for ourselves and some trouble wasn't our fault.

However, when you pray, you must believe God is working on your behalf and will change your story. Have faith that your prayers touched God, and His love for you is so vast that He will not allow your life to continue the same. God is rewriting your life; the prayers of the Righteous interceded on your behalf guarantees your past *won't be your story anymore.*

Have Faith . . .

Your life is about to change, God is writing a new narrative to inspire those who once knew of your struggle would now have to embrace your triumphant ascension. The expansion you prayed for, the money owed, returned, and His favor will speak on your behalf. Keep praying, keep seeking and never surrender to the taunts of the enemy.

God's word is the foundation of a new life. It's time to open your mind to receive what God has for you. Believe the word!!

Galatians 2:20—

"I have been crucified with Christ and I no longer live, but Christ lives in me. The life I now live in the body, I live by faith in the Son of God, who loved me and gave himself forme." You are a new creature, act like it.

Proverbs 3:5-6

"Trust in the Lord with all your heart and lean not to your own understanding. In all your ways acknowledge Him, and He shall direct your paths."

Remaining steadfast and dedicated in your faith

We must be careful and wise. The Bible is always true. Take advantage of new opportunities to strengthen your faith and create meaning in your everyday life.

Ephesians 5:15-16

"Be very careful, then, how you live — not as unwise but as wise, making the most of every opportunity, because the days are evil."

Jesus says that by dedicating yourself to Him, he will provide for you. Not only will He meet your spiritual needs, but He will meet some of your other tangible desires.

John 6:35

Then Jesus declared, "I am the bread of life. Whoever comes to me will never go hungry, and whoever believes in me will never be thirsty."

Remaining steadfast and dedicated in your faith allows you to lead by example. You must be open to direction from God, in order to continue being a good example of faith.

Proverbs 10:17

"Whoever heeds discipline shows the way to life, but whoever ignores correction leads others astray."

CHAPTER 8

PRAYER WILL SET YOU FREE

The Power of Prayer:

"And when he had apprehended him, he put him in prison, and delivered him to four quaternions of soldiers to keep him; intending after Easter to bring him forth to the people. Peter therefore was kept in prison: but prayer was made without ceasing of the church unto God for him. And when Herod would have brought him forth, the same night Peter was sleeping between two soldiers, bound with two chains: and the keepers before the door kept the prison. And behold, the angel of the Lord came upon him, and a light shined in the prison: and he smote Peter on the side, and raised him up, saying, Arise up quickly. And his chains felloff from his hands." **Acts 12:4-7 KJV**

This story is why we must know that prayer works. God has given us earthly stories with heavenly meaning to show His children the power of His being as *"I am Alpha and Omega, the beginning and the end"*. Men can't keep a bless man or woman bound. If your mind is blocked, you can be set free. This is the year to unlock yourself in your mind and release all negative energy and be who God called you to be. Romans 12:1-2, is the reason why you are free and can stay free. God can use you right where you are in life.

Don't ever allow anyone or anything to dissuade you from believing in God or miracles. An angel of the lord is assigned to you and will work with you and you must look up to receive the blessings of the Father.

I want to share a brief story about living fearful... I was over by fear when I received a diagnosis that I had cervical cancer. It was a difficult period emotionally, but it was also when I learned to trust God more and to pray effectively. I not only prayed for myself, but I prayed others through... being an intercessor is hard work, but it is transformational.

When you hear that type of news, saved or not you begin to think the worst. We all need a greater source of strength to pray you through. When I explained to the spiritual mothers of the church, they came together and formed a prayer group. Prayer was their main focus and knowing that when we pray together, there is power! In the scriptures, Peter needed a miracle to show the people that the God he believed would set him free ...The bible said that "prayer was made without ceasing of the church unto God for him." We also must have a greater belief in prayer... The pandemic of 2020 should inspire us to establish a relationship with the Lord and strive to have an effective prayer life so when tragedy strikes, and it will, your heart is not overwhelmed with fear and uncertainty. Being prayed up as the old saints use to say will cause you to be on the offense . . . taking back territory, casting out demons, laying hands on the sick, raising the dead. Miracles followed by signs and wonders become common. So, let us learn to pray without ceasing.

Another benefit in being prayed up is the ease to flow in the spirit realm. We need spiritual freedom to tap into spiritual dimensions to bring physical change in the earth, and this can only be achieved when we are in sync with the Holy Spirit.

If you try to pray and have malice or any other ill will in your heart you are operating in the flesh and the devil controls the atmosphere. Spiritual power is the only application that will defeat the antics of the enemy.

Prayer will set us free! Peter was set free and the prayer wheel just kept on turning on his behalf. *"Let's continue to pray for our own families, churches, and the world! Stay on the Prayer Wheel!"*

CHAPTER 9

PRAY, BELIEVE and KEEP
the FAITH

In the word of God, we are admonished how to apply our faith.

1 Corinthians 2:5-12 KJV: *"That your faith should not stand in the wisdom of men, but in the power of God. [6] Howbeit we speak wisdom among them that are perfect: yet not the wisdom of this world, nor of the princes of this world that come to nought: [7] But we speak the wisdom of God in a mystery, even the hidden wisdom, which God ordained before the world unto our glory: [8] Which none of the princes of this world knew: for had the deep things of God.*

[11] For what man knoweth the things of a man, save the spirit of man which is in him? even so the things of God knoweth no man, but the Spirit of God. [12] Now we have received, not the spirit of the world, but the spirit which is of God; that we might know the things that are freely given to us of God."

As I read those scripture verses my spirit began to pray. It is a common practice of humans to test things; we construct many feelers to see if something is of God and over analyze to the point of missing the move of the Spirit. We can be comforted in knowing that God always pave a way for his Children when we pray. He will never allow you to remain stuck and unfulfilled. His word has already declared that we are WINNERS! When we obey, the word keeps us on target because it's God's direction for our natural and spiritual life.

I am so grateful that God put people to speak a word in my life to let me know that I can have wisdom and become His chosen child. Your life is not up to man but lies in the power of God.

We have *God's* authority to declare and decree in prayer by faith the things that God has for us. His word made us a promise that "the spirit which is of God enables us to freely know what has been given to us of God."

IT'S YOURS FOR THE ASKING

The word also tells us that the wisdom we have is given by God not man, *BUT* we must ask for it. God's word is infallible; there is no failure. So, we must believe when we pray that things will continue to move in our favor and open opportunities for us and others. The time is now to get in position to pray so we can change this world that man thinks he has more wisdom than God. You are a spiritual giant when you pray and keep the faith. You might not see the manifestation *immediately*, but just believe it's already done.

Once I was in a very abusive relationship, I prayed so hard for God to get me out of this situation and if he did, I would serve Him until I die. That was my promise . . . During this time, I remember hearing a preacher on the radio say, "this might be your last time." Truly I knew that word was specifically for me to move.

I, perhaps just like you at some point in life fell to my weaknesses. I was in sin; I knew the right way to God but had lost confidence in myself. I hid from God. But one day I heard a word of faith that changed my life. Positive manifestations started when I rededicated my life back to Christ. I remember going to Christian Tabernacle and realigning myself in the word and made a promise to live for God. For holiness.

My faith was activated, and I got out of that abusive situation by the grace of God. Prayer was the principal element that defended me, that kept the devil from killing me from cervical cancer and prayer built a hedge me in an abusive home. The grace God allotted me paved an opening to leave; a small window of opportunity and it was exactly what I needed.

Let us remain hopeful and invest time in prayer; prayer is the key that causes our spiritual man to line up with the word of God. Prayer is the defense that keeps your adversary from overtaking you.

I know that my family was praying for me and they never gave up that's why it is important to continue praying for one another. It is a matter of life or death.

CHAPTER 10

YOU ARE A POWER SOURCE

"And he sought God in the days of Zechariah, who had understanding in the visions of God: and as long as he sought the Lord, God made him to prosper."2 Chronicles 26:5 KJV

In this chapter I want you to know that you are a power source. It has been over one year in this pandemic, and some of you have become the prayer lifeline for so many people. Some have tapped into the power source of prayer, just like electricity. And an added benefit to you is when you pray for others, what you petition for others God answers for you as well.

WHAT IS POWER?

Power means the ability to do something or act in a particular way, or the ability to direct or influence the behavior of others. Source means a place, person, or thing from which something comes or can be obtained.

When we pray, we become the praying source that God can utilize as conduits/vessels of change to set the captive free from spiritual bondage.

Prayer gives you power to pull down spiritual wickedness and strongholds against your life, family, finances, health, and destiny. This is why the enemy fights to distract the saints from praying, to keep them out of alignment with the power source. Have you noticed every time you commit to pray what happens; distraction, after distraction rapidly materializes? However, don't be disheartened, this is only a stronghold that you have authority and power over to defeat so look up and start praying.

It's time to help raise up more powerful young warriors and let them know that they have the strength and abilities to get a prayer through. Teaching others to pray will keep the prayer wheel moving. Don't be afraid to activate the gifts that God placed in you.

Some of you have felt the prayer wheel flow in your belly and shut it down, but now I am asking God to turn on the power source. To light fire in your belly to pray. Get ready for your prayer shock of the Holy Ghost!!

Prepare yourself in prayer to receive what God is going to release in your spirit. Get in to position and open your heart, don't retreat from the frontline, stand. Stand with confidence you are not fighting alone and go to war!

When the Dynamics Change

The Bible speaks about dwelling in that secret place of the most high. Our secret place is now our homes.

Some Christians live lazy lives; there is no consistent prayer time, fasting or concentration to separate themselves for service in the Kingdom. Many lived behind the prayers of their Leader, but God shifted the atmosphere with Covid-19 and forced us to look in the mirror and see what we're made of... Are we conquerors or quitters?

Each of us had to be our own prayer leader and warrior of the house... there was no place to run. This process was most difficult for those without a prayer altar in their home, but for those of us who have dedicated time and space to God we learned to press in harder, and war against dark spiritual influences plaguing our nation.

We knew and understood God is in control of everything that goes on from the White House to the Church house. So, we locked in and pressed through the mine fields of doubt, sickness, lack, and yes, a Pandemic.

Understanding how essential prayer is to living victorious in the world, I pray that God has gotten the church's attention. We must not miss the hand of God in this season. This is our season to walk in integrity, accountability, dependability, and faithfulness to God, not to man.

What's Next?

Similarly, to the woman that persisted with the unjust Judge in scripture and prevailed because of her tenacity and unwillingness to give up, we must know God has power, and that He will release that power to change our situation if we persist.

Likewise, we must have the same spirit in this season in order for God to do His work through us. God needs us to pray the world into the next dimension of power and steadfastness.

The question I ask, "ARE YOU READY" CAN GOD TRUST YOU?

Prayer is a Petition

When we learn the power and purpose of making petitions to God, we will operate in a fuller manifestation of personal power in the earth.

What is a Petition?

Petition is a legal appeal or demand on a Government based on Constitutional Rights protected by law. And as covenanted children with rights and privileges God is appealing to us to stand up and take our rightful place in the world spiritually and naturally. We can make an *effective* difference when we fall down on our "KNEES" and incorporate "FASTING AND PRAYING" consistently. This has to be a lifestyle, not an event.

8 Watches . . .

The Bible speaks of watches, which are precise times of the day or night in which you pray.

I really want your soul to be blessed by this...

Though many churches do not teach extensively about the different Watches, there is a strategy designed to set you apart from lukewarm individuals and ministries.

Essentially, eight watches cover *24-hours* in the day. Every prayer watch has a targeted goal. This is why you may find yourself frequently led to pray at particular times of the day or evening. These 8 prayer watches are referred to as "the watch of the Lord" or "watching in prayer." The 8 prayer watches are the patterns displayed in the life of Jesus to have heaven invade the earth.

When we enter our prayer closets, we partner with the Father, the Son, and Holy Spirit to see the kingdom's purpose come upon the land and spread throughout the earth. In various accounts of the gospels, Jesus invited His disciples to watch with Him in prayer. He wanted them to stay awake naturally to pray and to also watch spiritually in prayer to avoid the traps and snares that leads to temptation.

If you have ever been awakened during the night or are wondering why you are being led to pray at specific times, it is almost certainly because God wants you to pray or intercede for someone or something. Romans 8:14, tells us, "For those who are led by the Spirit of God are the children of God." At times, we willingly and unwillingly fail to obey the voice and leading of the Holy Spirit. Don't resist the urge to pray or give in to the temptation to draw back in prayer.

Jesus desires to see groups of two or more gathered in His name, asking in one voice and in one heart for His will to be done. He said, "I tell all of you with certainty that if two of you agree on earth about anything you request, it will be done for you by my Father in heaven. For where two or three have gathered together in My name, there I am in their midst" |Matthew 18:18-20|. Unity in prayer is the heart of the "Watch of the Lord."

I had to learn how to become a prayer meeting in myself. You must be able to get a prayer to God at any time of the day and night. You must know how to make your petition to God when you are in need, God will hear your cry. You must learn to get in the face of God and just you and Him in the prayer meeting alone.

It is important that you know His word while

you are praying. The word confirms, heals, delivers and sets us free. You must believe! God's word is preparing His people for greatness, destiny, and purpose. The word lets us know that this way is already made for his people.

Scriptures regarding Preparation

Ezekiel 38:7 ASV

"Be prepared, and prepare yourself, you and all your companies that are assembled about you and be a guard for them".

John 14:3 ASV

And if I go and prepare a place for you, I will come again and receive you to Myself, that where I am, there you may be also".

Psalm 23:5 ASV

"Thou preparest a table before me in the presence of my enemies;Thou have anointed my head with oil; My cup runneth over".

Exodus 23:20 ASV

"Behold, I am going to send an angel before you to guard you along the way and to bring you into the place which I have prepared".

My Foundation . . .

I will never forget at the age of three years old, living in Chester, Pennsylvania. My grandmother, Evangelist Reba P. Richardson Jackson, was the church mother of the church, New Light Community Praise Center in Delaware, she was 92-year-old. She was a serious praying woman... Grandmother had twenty-two children and took her final rest one month prior she would've turned 93 years-old.

My grandmother would pick me up from preschool and around three-o'clock, we would go to one of her friend's house where there were other women in the front room praying. They would say, "Reba, someday Darlinda will be a young prayer warrior". I was so afraid and didn't understand why they were saying that about me.

However, as I was growing up I found myself imitating what they were doing. I would get my dolls and line them up and I would start praying. It is true that you lead by the examples you see and learn. Even though I went astray when I became older, I still found myself praying in the worst situations of my life. I just believe that Prayer prepared the way for me. I found myself right back to my first love, "JESUS".

Just know that you will have your own encounters with God. Your life is your testimony and you will find yourself on your knees crying out to the Lord.

There are prayer principles that we must follow in life. Remember, without God, man cannot, and without man God will not. What happens on earth depends on you. Prayer is an earthly license for heavenly interference. Prayer is not an option but a necessity.

Chapter 11

PRAYER PAVES THE WAY

(Bishop Reuben Timothy Jones)

I am the biological son of the late Mother R.T. Jones Sr., and spiritual grandson of the late Mother Juanita Dabney, so I've been both a victim and benefactor of prayer all the years of my life that I can remember. You may ask why am I a victim of prayer? I believe many people suffer from this syndrome, due to a misconception of what prayer really is. Prayer is simply an expression of the heart's desire, be it spoken or unexpressed.

Having said this, we treat God like a Santa Claus or an Easter Bunny, always with our hands out and asking for the newest toy or the fanciest clothes, so forth and so on. We use prayer as a platform to get what we want.

As a young boy growing up in church, this was my attitude. Next, if I'd done something, I know I shouldn't have done, my prayer, Lord please don't let mom and dad find out. My most famous prayer had to do with a set of trains I wanted for Christmas, man I prayed, and I prayed, I prayed all night long; you know how the song went. When I got up Christmas morning, there was a train set, it wasn't the one I wanted. Here was my first remembered disappointment. I thought prayer was just simply asking and receiving what I wanted, when I wanted, never ever considering God's will.

One of the areas to consider is that too often when we pray, we insert the words, Lord if it's your will. My perspective on that is, we are now inserting doubt into our prayers by saying IF. In my experience, I use the phrases, according to Your will let it be so, or simply in Your will Father we pray. Be advised concerning the sovereignty of God. Matt 6:8 Your Father knows what you need before you ask Him. In the next verse, He gives a pattern, which we call the Lord's prayer, to use when we pray. Notice the emphasis, Thy will be done on earth as it is in heaven. There are no conjectures here. The will of God is definite.

Therefore, when I pray it's either in or according to the will of God. I'm never disappointed because of the outcome of my prayers because I've submitted it to the will of God, and not to my will. In 1972, my only son, at the time developed a terminally ill disease and died. The whole family prayed consistently for God to spare his life. Yes, we were saddened when he passed. We ultimately knew the will of God had been accomplished.

When he was born, I was in the military and had received orders to go to Vietnam. My son was my ticket out of the military. I received a hardship discharge because of him. He lived 5 years and died. He fulfilled his mission. We learn that God is not a puppet, with us as puppet masters, pulling the strings. God is always in control even when we are out of control.

1Thes. 5:17-18 admonishes us to pray without ceasing, and in everything give thanks for this is the will of God in Christ Jesus concerning you. I make the special reference, the scripture doesn't say thank God for everything, but in everything. To me that says, find a way in every situation to give God thanks. Prayer then becomes a matter of lifestyle.

Luke 18:1 "And He spake a parable unto them that men ought always to pray and not to faint". To me that says we must always be in a prayerful mindset. No, we are not on our knees 24 hours a day, neither are we bowing our heads 24 hours a day. We are like an automobile *engaged* in the drive mode, so that any moment our minds can connect with God through instantaneous prayer. We don't have to think about it, it's automatic.

The critical lesson learned is, He's not our Santa Claus, neither is He our Easter Bunny, nor is He a genie in the bottle. The great disappointment comes when we wake up to realize that prayer isn't simply about us asking God for things. This is when Matthew 16:26 NIV, comes alive "What good will it be for someone to gain the whole world, yet forfeit their soul?" In our Christian development these are crucial lessons we learn. The fact that we were to Ask, and it shall be given, Seek and you will find, Knock and the door will open, there are so many other principles we must add to that. So, then our approach to prayer must be different. Prayer is not simply a matter of praying for things to satisfy the flesh.

The flesh is always seeking to be satisfied, to be gratified, glorified, and exalted. This is why I have a personal problem with prophets, so called, who are always promising bigger cars, better jobs, bigger homes, bigger bank accounts, always prophesying good fortunes to the people of God, neglecting the fact that many are the afflictions of the righteous, understanding that God does deliver them out of them all. In the story of Job who was righteous, who was perfect in his generation, lost everything, and cursed the very day he was born. Yes, all was restored, he received double for his trouble. He had to suffer much before gaining much.

So, the real lesson in prayer comes when you hit a brick wall, that's where you feel God has not heard you and God is not answering. This comes as a result of us believing God is standing by waiting for you to ask for more things; when in effect God is waiting for you to offer more of you to Him. Let me stop for a moment to say God always answers prayer in one of three ways. **1-yes, 2-no, 3-wait**. Our trouble many times is our unwillingness to accept any answer but yes. Too often when the negative or "wait" becomes the answer, too many will not give God the credit for the no or the wait; and be satisfied to say I'm still waiting for God banswer. If you really think about it, how many times have you said I haven't gotten my answer from God yet?

We must be ready to accept the sovereignty of an omniscient God. God shares with man His Omnipotence. He says when the Holy Ghost has come upon you, you shall have power to cast out devils. He doesn't share His omniscience to the same degree. Surely the Lord will do nothing except He reveal it to His servant the prophet Amos 3:7. He shares His power with the Spirit filled; His omniscience with His prophets. Got knows what will happen before it happens, and reveal it to His prophet, whom He describes as His servant.

One of the most shocking experiences I had with prayer came in 1966. There I was serving in the military in Columbia, SC. The now Bishop Howard Crosby, who had been a schoolmate of mine since Jr High, convinced me to attend a church at 2222 Barnhamville Rd. I had grown up in Christian Tabernacle, my mom was the prayer leader. She would pray and we all followed her lead. In this church, The Progressive Church of the Lord Jesus Christ, at the prayer meeting, there was no prayer leader. It appeared to be a free for all meeting. I was baffled, no one was setting the tone, no one took the lead, and everyone was calling out to the Lord in their own way. No, I didn't question it, I just fell in line.

What I learned from that experience was that every person had to meet God at their specific level and learn to pray through for oneself. It taught me to respect the different methods to gaining access to the throne of God.

Hebrews 4:16, admonishes us to come boldly unto the throne of grace, that we may obtain mercy and find grace to help in time of need.

As I move forward on the subject of prayer, I've already stated that prayer is the sincere heart's/soul's desire, uttered or unexpressed. As I consider this, it is not the end of the story.

As a young man growing up there was a radio series hosted by Paul Harvey titled "*The Rest of the Story*". He would give the news as written, then would say "Now here's the rest of the story." On this matter of prayer let me quote Paul Harvey, "Now here's the Rest of the Story." Prayer in too many instances has become too many people simply talking to themselves. Laying out a platform for all the things they want or like to see.

Lord, if you please Sir Master, do this for me, do that for me, make a way out of no way. Heal my mother, deliver my father, protect my children, on and on, ending by saying, "If you do that for me Jesus I'll be careful to give your name the praise, amen. I've always been taught that prayer is a dialogue with God. Unfortunately, we've made it a monologue. We do all the talking, never letting God speak to us. Then we become frustrated when it appears our prayers are unheard or unanswered.

We are satisfied if our needs are met; or that our prayers are answered. We never take the time to consider where God is in all of this. Our prayers are selfish and *one-sided*, and full of, what I call the me factor. If you do that for me Jesus, I'll be satisfied, I'll give your name all the praise, glory, and honor. When do these types of prayers become a dialogue, or a conversation between you and God? When is God allowed to speak while you're praying? When, for that matter, is God permitted to answer your request? I call these *presumptuous* prayers.

We presume that because of our selfish faith, that God is duty bound to answer in the fashion in which we've asked. Never, in our wildest imagination do we expect a **NO** from God. We are like children in a candy store. Gimme œof those, and one of these, so forth and so on. Never considering that our prayers should always be in and according to the will of God through Jesus Christ our Lord.

We are situationally unaware, not present in mind and spirit, and like *clockwork* when things don't go our way, the question then becomes where God in all of this is. I must note here, that when we come before God in prayer, it should be a time when we listen to also gain direction from the throne of grace. Heb 4:16 CEV "So whenever we are in need, we should come bravely before the throne of our merciful God. There we will be treated with undeserved grace and will find help". If we expect God to help us, we must be willing to listen to the instructions He gives us through our prayers.

What I am saying is that we need to develop a way of praying where we talk then listen to the direction of the Spirit. Seeking God's will in every endeavor.

Before I can continue, I must say there are several different types or means of prayer.

Every Sunday morning at church there is an Invocation. I imagine the question then arises, what in the world is an invocational prayer? This is a prayer generally given at the beginning of a service, a public ceremony seeking and entreating God for guidance, protection, inspiration, etc. This is done or at least should be done every wakening day of our lives, as we go about our daily business.

We then have prayers of supplication, which is a prayer of petitioning God by asking for whatever is needed at the time for self or for someone else. We can hear the people praying, "Send on your help Lord, make a way, let the healing hand of God be upon this situation, that situation, or whatever the situation may be".

The prayer of Faith; the bible says that the prayer of faith will save the sick. All prayers are prayed in faith, believing that God hears and answers prayer. I must add again here that no prayer ever goes unanswered. The problem is that the answer isn't always in the positive Many times, we consider a *negative* answer a no answer. As we are His sheep, and the sheep of His pasture, we must accept the answers as His will at the time.

Prayers of Thanksgiving. This is when we thank God for everything and ask for nothing. Someone said the safest place in the whole wide world, is in the will of God. Sometimes that will land us in the middle of a storm. The thanksgiving comes because God shows up and sends deliverance in the midst of the storm. We must learn to thank God in good times and bad. If He takes you to it; He can and will bring you through it. Phil 4:6 will help us here.

Prayers of Worship, this prayer causes us to recognize who God is as opposed to prayers of thanksgiving, where we thank God for what He has done.

Prayers of Consecration; this is a time of setting ourselves apart from all to seek the will of God. As a child growing up in church, my mother would gather many people the 1st weekend of every month from Friday night to Sunday night after worship in what was known as Consecration weekend prayer.

I didn't understand the value of it then; the years have taught me the value of consecration and setting myself aside to seek the willof God, not for my life, but for the moment. Each season of life brings about different challenges. After 60 years in ministry, I recognize that there is life after pastoring. We must recognize when one season is over to make room for another season in life and the ministry, all according to the will of God.

The Prayer of Imprecation, unfortunately it's hard for some to recognize that prayer should not be used as an offensive wedding. God is not a pit bull to sick on people that whichannoy us or attack us. The prayer of imprecation which we see in the Psalms, where it emphasizes the holiness of God, His mercy and His love. In Matt. 5 we pray God's blessings and not curses upon our enemies.

When we pray, we must pray in the Spirit, even when we don't have adequate words to express ourselves. Romans 8:26 teaches us "Likewise the Spirit also helpeth our infirmities:

for we know not what we should pray for as we ought: but the Spirit itselfmaketh intercession for us with groanings which cannot be uttered."

Prayers is Conversation with God and should be made without ceasing. When you love something, it's your desire to communicate with the one you love. I don't understand people who never communicate with God, whom they testify they love.

Jesus, in what we call The Lord's Prayer, sets the tone for the pattern used as we pray. Sometimes, there are prayers even in the hymns we sing. My favorite, Lord Jesus I long to be perfectly whole; I want Thee forever to live in my soul, break down every idle, cast out every foe, now wash me and I shall be whiter than snow. Lord Jesus look down from Thy throne in the sky, help me to make a complete sacrifice; I give up myself and whatever I know, now wash me and I shall be whiter than snow. Whiter than snow, ye whiter than snow; now wash me and I shall be whiter than snow.

Let us look at prayer as it relates to faith. The bible says that the prayer of faith will save the sick

(James 5th chapter). Hebrews 11, "Now faith is the substance of things hoped for; the evidence of things not seen". Having examined these and other faith scriptures, sometimes we are still confused. The reason for the confusion is because when we pray, we pray in the will and according to the will of GOD.

The key word here is FAITH. Hebrews 11 gives a guide to what faith is. Faith makes us sure of what we hope for and gives us proof of what we cannot see. The fundamental fact of existence is that trust in God, this faith, is the firm foundation under everything that makes life worth living.

Now faith is the assurance of things hoped for, a conviction of things not seen. When I went to Webster's dictionary, firm belief in something for which there is no proof. Complete trust, without question. There is also an archaic transitive verb for faith; Believe, Trust. While we claim faith as a noun, it is important that we also recognize faith as a verb. As a verb it causes us to live our faith by how we treat others. How we vote, handle finance and business, how we rear our children. Faith then becomes how we go about our daily lives. I call it faith in action, which then causes us to take the gospel to the world. In this sense it rises from being archaic to the realm of activism.

When I read the bible in the 14th chapter of Matthew, Peter prays; "Lord if it be thou upon the waters, bid me to come unto thee upon the waters." And He said come. And Peter went down from the boat and walked upon the waters to come to Jesus. Notice they are still in the midst of a storm.

However, in verse 30, but when he saw the wind boisterous, he was afraid; and beginning to sink, he cried out, saying, "Lord, save me". I thought I'd use this story as a defining moment for prayer, faith, and the power of Jesus to save in the midst of the storm. We must understand that Peter was in the boat with the other 11 disciples when the storm developed. They saw a person walking on the water, whom they didn't initially recognize. When Jesus said come, Peter was the only one to step out of the boat. When you pray, you must never concern yourself about the people around you. Sometimes you must stand alone upon your faith and conviction.

Notice, Peter began walking on the water, doing what was impossible. God gives power to the faint, and to those who have no might He increases strength. As he is walking, the bible says, when he saw the wind boisterous, he was afraid and beginning to sink he cried out "Lord save me."

In this life, there are many storms, many distractions, from without and from within. The fact remains we must, above all else, hold on to faith and courage that the Lord is with you, and will save you, in the midst of the storm. Jesus saved Peter in the storm. Faith says that God doesn't out to deliver you from the storm; He can deliver you in the storm. The storm didn't cease until they were both in the boat. The disciples had to ask the question what kind of man is this, that even the winds and the waves obey him.

When you pray in faith, with the understanding that God knows and understands all about your struggles, He will guide our every footstep to deliver us and bring us safe to the shore. Prayer plus faith equals unlimited power and results.

The hymnologist said My faith looks up to Thee, Thou lamb of calvary Savior divine. Now hear me while I pray, take all my sins away, Lord let me from this day, by wholly Thine. May Thy rich grace impart, strength to my fainting heart, my zeal inspire; as Thou has died for me, oh may my love to Thee pure warm and changeless be a living fire.

How often have we heard these expressions concerning prayer? Prayer Works, More things are wrought through prayer than the world has ever dreamed possible. Prayer changes things. Much prayer, much power; little prayer, little power. The devil can't harm a praying man.

Pray when things go wrong, prayer will keep you ever strong. Did you stop to pray this morning? As children at bedtime, we generally learned one of two prayers, which went something like this, "Now I lay me down to sleep, I pray the Lord my soul to keep; If I should die before I wake, I pray the Lord my soul to take." Or we recited the Lord's prayer. Of course, at the end of the prayer, we'd ask the Lord to bless, by naming the family, closing out with bless everybody everywhere, Amen.

These nightly prayers, at least, taught us a sense of the value of praying each night to finish out our day.

As I look back on those expressions, sayings, maybe even cliches concerning prayer, I have to ask myself, what was the underlying causes that brought about these sayings. Were there some elements that were missed? I think what we must incorporate into each of those saying is FAITH. We've been taught that without faith it is impossible to please God. We learn from Hebrews 11(Amplified) "Now faith is the assurance (*title deed, confirmation*) of things hoped for (*divinely guaranteed*) and the evidence of things not seen [the conviction of their *reality-faith* comprehends as fact what cannot be experienced by the physical senses].

For by this [*kind of*] faith the men of old gained [divine] approval. Note, without faith, it is impossible to please God. James 5:16(AMPC) The earnest (heartfelt, continued) prayer of a righteous man makes tremendous power available [dynamic in its working]. (KJV) The effectual fervent prayer of a righteous man availeth much."

Now the question becomes, what is the effectual fervent prayer? We, at first sight understand that it must mean some sort of energy displayed here. Is there a sense of enthusiasm on display? I believe in our prayers, there must be a sense of urgency; we cannot have an attitude of, I've tried everything else, let me now try God. We may lack alot of the world's goods; we may not have the riches of many. We must understand that the fervor and effectiveness of our prayers brings the power of God into our circumstance. It isn't how long nor how loud we pray; it is our persistent and consistent prayer that makes the difference.

We must learn that the prayer of others is always good. It is not until we learn to apply prayer to our personal lives, will we ever truly experience the value of what it means to pray through.

We are living in difficult times. Our worship is now through social media. I think that the almighty must have known these days would come. The writer of Hebrews 10:24-25. *"And let us consider one another to provoke unto love and to good works: Not forsaking the assembling of ourselves together, as the manner of some is, and so much the more, as ye see the day approaching".* For several months now, many churches have been forced to close doors because of a pandemic. The gathering now is through *Zoom,* social media by means of *Facebook,* Twitter, *Instagram,* etc.

During this time, our prayer should be even so come Lord Jesus. This is the time when the people of God should put into practice, everything we have ever learned about the power of prayer; knowing that God sees and knows all about our struggles. The Psalmist reminds us that weeping endures for a night, but joy comes in the morning. Keep pushing, lean in harder . . . *change is coming.*

Now once we understand that God's time clock isn't like ours the *process* gets easier. Moses in the 90th Psalm reminds us that a thousand years with God is as a day. That tells me that in God's timing we are only minutes from our joy coming.

Though WE get old and tired, Time doesn't get old, neither does it ever get tired. A day is still

24 hours, a year is still 365 days, 366 in the leap year. Time doesn't complain, it just keeps on moving. This is really how our prayers should be, constant and consistent Lord let your will be done on earth as it is in heaven. Once we learn to accept God's will, be it yea, nay, or wait, our lives will become more meaningful. Please never lose sight on the words of the hymn "Thy way oh Lord, not mine. Thou will be done, not mine".

Since thou for me didst bleed, and now doth intercede, each day I simply plead, Thy will be done.

If I take a walk and look at the life of Christian Tabernacle, I take particular notice of the fact that prayer and fasting was an integral part of the ministry. Bishop and Mother Jones made sure that the church as a hole, and the youth specifically remained consistently in prayer. Never did a holiday past by and we were note in church. It's interesting to note that we brought our picnic baskets to church on holidays. The amazing part about it, was the fact that the teenagers of that day never complained about the prayers and brought in church on holidays. Yes, we prepared our lunches, packed them up and went to church for a day of self-denial. We prayed, had fellowship, and fun all at the same event at the church house. As I think about it today, I'm not sure whether the youth of today would be able to stand the regimentation of the 50s and 60s.

The youth of that day were disciplined to be in church every holiday. Prayer, fasting, and consecration was the focus of our lives. That's not to say we didn't have our challenges. Yes, we messed up, got into trouble for disobedience from time to time. In the end, because of Mother's prayers and Bishop's preaching we survived.

The original theme of the church was "*Trust Him Today.*" In the late 1950s, early 1960s, Bishop changed the theme of the church to "*I Believe God*". Bishop stressed, that even when people called our homes, we answered with these words, "I Believe God. Even today, if you call my number, I yet answer with the words "I Believe God." Through the power of prayer, telephone greetings, I Believe God. Oh, don't let me forget Monday night hour of power.

Every Monday night at 7pm, the church would be in prayer. Even today, we are in prayer nightly at 8pm. Prayer and Bible study led by Pastor Barmore Tuesday Nights at 8:00pm. Prayer is yet the foundation upon which our Church, Christian Tabernacle had always been known as a church built on the preached word of God, prayer and fasting. Next, it was the first weekend of the month our weekend shut in prayer and consecration. Many miracles of healing, and deliverance. We've even experienced God withholding the hand of death. I've seen sight restored to the blind.

The song *"Lord I want a deeper consecration, Lord I want a deeper consecration; Lord I want a deeper consecration, I want to loose myself in Thee"*, yet resonates in my spirit. I can still hear the Saints singing, "In my heart, in my heart, Lord send a great revival, teach me how to watch and pray, and to read my Bible".

Even though the seasons have changed, I still remember how the Saints remembered those days. Let me say that the foundation has been laid, men should always pray and not faint.

Chapter 12

HALLS OF ETERNITY

➢ These words spake Jesus, and lifted up his eyes to heaven, and said, Father, the huris come; **glorify thy Son**, that thy Son also may glorify thee.

➢ As thou hast given him power over all flesh, that he should give eternal life to as many as thou hast given him.

➢ And this is life eternal, that they might know thee the only true God, and Jesus Christ, whom thou hast sent.

➢ I have glorified thee on the earth: I have finished the work which thou gavest me to do.

➢ And now, O Father, glorify thou me with thine own self with the glory which I had with thee before the world was.

➢ I have manifested thy name unto the men which thou gavest me out of the world: thine they were, and thou gavest them me; and they have kept thy word.

➢ Now they have known that all things whatsoever thou hast given me are of thee.

➢ For I have given unto them the words which thou gavest me; and they have received them and have known surely that I came out from thee, and they have believed that thou didst send me.

➤ I pray for them: I pray not for the world, but for them which thou hast given me; for they are thine.

➤ And all mine are thine, and thine are mine; and I am glorified in them.

This is the most extensive and profound prayer of Jesus we have. It portrays a prayer of Jesus Christ addressed to His Father, placed in context immediately before His betrayal and crucifixion, the events which the gospel often refers to as His glorification.

In these verses, (1-4), He prayed for His glorification in Heaven (v. 5), and He prayed for His glorification in the church (2, 3, 10). We read John 17 we see that Jesus asked for 2 things: "To glorify Your Son, that He may glorify the Father" (v. 1-4) and to "Restore Your Son the His former glory".

We should realize that Jesus' intercession for his disciples from within God's presence anticipates his role after his ascension. This prayer has been known as the *High Priestly Prayer*. In his prayer Jesus will speak of the past and the future from an eternal perspective. Jesus now addresses the theme of glory, asking the Father to glorify theSon so that the Son may glorify the Father, but it is all grounded in the present, at this particular climatic point in salvation history.

Nevertheless, he prayed for the benefit of those present (11:41-42), and the same is true here as well (17:13). Jesus' whole life has been a revelation of the Father, based on Jesus' union with him, so it is appropriate that his teaching concludes in the form of prayer, the genre most closely associated with union with God.

We are one of God's disciples and we are part of the inheritance of this prayer. When I read the chapter, tears began to roll out my eyes because just knowing that Jesus prayed for me and now I am protected under His blood. I always believed even when I was in sin that

God was watching over me and the prayers were protecting me. I can remember a time when I was walking through a dirt trail, took a shortcut to a friend's house, and there was a man following me. I was so afraid, and I started walking faster, but I remember my Grandmother said to me, pray no matter what is happening.

So, I began to say the Lord's prayer out loud and that man went another way and stopped following me. There have been so many occasions in my life that I know that prayer prepared the way for me not to die before my time. We must know that Jesus' prayer is still with us today because He is sitting on the right hand of the Father advocating and praying for us.

We are in the times that you must know for sure that your prayers are being answered when you pray. You must stay in the presence of the Lord so He can hear your cries.

I believe that this prayer in comparing this text to the synoptic gospels and imagining the scene (Matthew, Mark, and Luke), it seems most likely to me that **John 17** was thecontinuation of Jesus' prayer in Gethsemane, which began in the synoptics with Jesusasking God to take away the cup of suffering but yielding to the Father's plan.

This is how much Jesus loves us and why he died for you and I. In verse 3, Jesus decided that he wasn't going to leave us alone before he was crucified on the cross. Jesus took the time and looked down the halls of eternity to make sure you and I would make it while left here in the cruel and wicked world. He made sure we knew the true God and gave us the opportunity to live in this world that He created. His word will never die and His prayer will also never die. That is why he lets us know that His prayers are for eternity, and you can have eternal life when you get to heaven.

Always know that Jesus is sitting on the right side of His father, still looking down the halls of eternity praying for you and me.

Chapter 13

I AM a PRAYER MEETING

I had to learn how to become a prayer meeting in myself. You must be able to get a prayer to God at any time of the day and night. You must know how to make your petition to God when you are in need. God will hear your cry. You must learn to get in the face of God and just you and Him in the prayer meeting alone.

I remember going to Christian Tabernacle, Philadelphia, PA. It was in the early 90's. We would have service every Thursday with the late Mother R.T. Jones, this was the time they would teach us about being a lady in the church, she told us to be a "Peach out of reach and not a Dum Plum," and taught us how to pray and get in God's face.

Meeting God in your secret place is music to His ears and melody to His heart. Once you are taught how to pray, you want to pray more and more. Having that one on one alone with God is peaceful and rewarding. You will see results and prayers are answered.

Typically, a prayer meeting is a group of lay people getting together for the purpose of prayer as a group. Prayer meetings are typically conducted inside or outside regular services by one or more members of the clergy or other forms of religious leadership, but they may also be initiated by decision of non-leadership members as well.

Since the Covid19 Pandemic 2020, you had to become your own prayer meeting, congregation, and the preacher. You didn't have time to call on the prayer leaders or the pastor, there were times when you needed God to come right now. You didn't have time to gather the people in the church because it's been closed since March 2020, or call a zoom, and go on Facebook live. Many times, you had to call a 911 prayer meeting for yourself and call on the name of Jesus. There were numerous times I had to fall down on my knees right where I was in my house and plead the blood of Jesus for my life and others.

It was a common practice (lifestyle) to have my own praise break, praise and worship service, and when the pandemic hit, my prayer life *intensified.*

I petitioned God fervently to have mercy on this world; Lord we need you right now, save this world from hell and destruction. We must continue to meet God in that secret place and plead the blood because the blood still works. We have a duty and a charge to pray earnestly. (James 5: 13-16) We have full instruction from the Bible. "Wake up"' no more sleeping on the job! Pray! Pray! Pray!

When you are home in your own prayer meeting, you should pray the way God gives it to you. Never try to be like anyone else.

I learned how to pray by talking to God myself. I have sat in so many prayer meetings and experienced the power of God *manifest in* the room and seeing the power of God heal, deliver, and set free.

Since we have been in this pandemic, I remember laboring in those *all-night* prayer meetings at Christian Tabernacle where I first saw the light in 1992. That was the start of my *prayer-life* and I hungered and thirsted after *uprightness.* I witnessed the late Mother R.T Jones, sitting on the prayer altars for others and call down fire from heaven in the prayer meeting. The hunger of God was upon me ever since. I saw the prayer warriors and intercessors, warrioring in the spirit for another soul. That was one of my greatest prayer times because I was introduced to God in a prayer meeting.

Now, I know how to enter into the realm of the spirit of God alone and hold on to the Horns of the Altar for others.

When you hunger for God, for His touch, when pray, you will not hold back while you are praying. The *fervency* will flow out of your belly and the Holy Spirit will move and feel like fire. You must learn how to sit among the prayer warriors and know the spirit of God. This is serious and God is about His business when He needs you to be on the front line battling for his people. You have to make your election sure if you are going to be a truefrontline prayer warrior and intercessor. We are needed in the prayer kingdom. You cannot be afraid to enter into the warrior room. You are going to fight some heavy battles and cast out many demons.

The question you need to ask yourself is, can I stand in the heat of the battle? Ephesians 6:10, will prepare you for this prayer journey.

This is the prayer that was upon me as I was writing this chapter, this is real! I felt the Holy Spirit come upon me strongly and I began to pray. I couldn't put all the prayer on paper as it was coming out!

As I begin to pray: Father God in the name of Jesus, we blessed thine name for blessing us. I come before you humbly as I know how. Forgive me for all my sins and cleanse me from all of my unrighteousness and create in me a clean heart. Thank you Jesus for sparing me another day, I come on behalf of others. I just want to tell you thank you God for looking over your people everywhere. Touch, heal, deliver and set free. God this is the day that the Lord has made, we shall rejoice and be glad in it. Oh, magnify the Lord with me and let us exalt his name together. God I come standing in need of prayer. Father, I come on today interceding for others asking You to stretch out your mighty hand, God let your healing come upon this land today. God break up every *fallow* ground that caused people to don't want to know you.

I pray for souls on today that God they will hear your word and come back and say yes I repent. God send your healing on today, the world is in need of healing mentally, in their souls today, glory to your name, glory to your name. Oh God I thank you father for what you already have done.

I speak to the wind and command it to obey the word of the Lord. Let the wind blow upon your people today; *call the sun to shine and cause the water to behave.* God I know you're able to do exceedingly above all that we can ask for, please God bless your people in a special way. Jesus look upon your people everywhere, look upon our children, look upon our family members, look upon our seniors on today, look upon all the saints of God all over this world. This is a 911 call for your help!!

I thank you and I praise you for answering my prayer on this day, let the words of my mouth and the meditation of my heart be acceptable in your sight oh Lord, my strength and my redeemer. Amen

Ask God to teach you how to pray so you can get a prayer through. Keep PRAYING! No time to quit! Pray for God to give you a PRAYING SPIRIT!

In closing, remember these words from a song the church sang when I was a little boy: **"Don't stop praying . . ."**

Conclusion

Your prayers will *never* die. God's ears will always be upon the righteous. We are needed in the kingdom as intercessors, prayer warriors, and soldiers. We must remain on the battlefield in prayer. Until you go to eternity you must never stop praying. I have shown you in John 17, Jesus prayed until the very hour they came to take Him for His last journey. You will know when you are about to reach your last mission on earth. God warns us to get our house in order. His word is truth, and He is preparing us through His word so that we can see Him in glory if we just believe. The prayers of Jesus have prepared the way! We must never give up praying and must keep the faith when we pray.

Prayer is neither official nor formal or ceremonial, but direct, hearty, intense. Prayer is not religious; it is like a needy child crying out for his father for mercy, so he can have compassion on him. When you ask God in prayer you expect to get an answer. The aim is to seek and you shall find, the purpose of knocking is to arouse attention and get in, and this is why you must pray without ceasing.

I realize that we must continue to teach our next generation why it is important to pray. The lesson of prayer needs to be emphasized, iterated and reiterated in the ears of people during this modern time, and bear with cumulative force on each generation. We must teach them to seek and pray to God with their whole heart and have vision of conscience for eternal things, though many presently have deaf ears toward God. Nothing is nearly never more important to God than prayer in dealing with mankind, because failing to pray is failure along the entire line of life. It is a failure of our duty, service, and spiritual progress if we don't pray.

In James chapter 1, verses 1-8. (NIV), James is giving us a Salutation. This means the act of saluting, a greeting; the act of paying respect or reverence by the customary words or actions.

See examples:

1 James, a servant of God and of the Lord Jesus Christ, to the twelve tribes scattered among the nations: Greetings.

2 Consider it pure joy, my brothers and sisters, whenever you face trials of many kinds, because you know that the testing of your faith produces perseverance.

3 Let perseverance finish its work so that you may be mature and complete, not lacking anything.

4 If any of you lacks wisdom, you should ask God, who gives generously to all without finding fault, and it will be given to you.

5 But when you ask, you must believe and not doubt, because the one who doubts is like a wave of the sea, blown and tossed by the wind.

6 That person should not expect to receive anything from the Lord.

7 Such a person is double-minded and unstable in all they do.

We must continue to realize that God's word will always be true and Jesus will always walk with us until eternity.

TOOLS FOR PRAYER

QUESTIONS ABOUT PRAYING.

1. What does prayer mean to you?

2. How often do you pray?

3. How can you enhance your prayer life?

4. Do you have faith in God when you pray?

Make prayer part of your lifestyle.

Establish a time and place for your prayer time. (Mark 1:35)

Write down your prayer time.

Have paper or a tablet when you're praying.

Prepare yourself to pray

1. Ask for forgiveness! (Repent) 1 John 1:9 & Isaiah 59:2

2. Pray from the heart (James 4:3)

3. You pray in Jesus' name (John 14;13-14)

4. Pray for others (1 Thes. 5:25)

Create A Prayer List

Notes:

_____

_____

_____

_____

_____

_____

_____

_____

_____

_____

_____

_____

About the Authors

Darlinda Turner is an ordained minister and has been pastoring with her husband, Pastor Claret Turner for sixteen years at the New Light Community Praise Center, located in downtown Wilmington, Delaware. They have been married for 20 years.

In addition, Darlinda has been blessed to serve and lead on many levels through her involvement in various ministries. The mission of her ministry, "Women on the Battlefield," is to bless hurting women and stand on the front line for their souls as Prayer Warriors.

Her mentors were the late Mother Reba R. Jackson, Mother R.T. Jones, Mother Winne Hightower, and Mother Marlene Tally. These women were great Pioneers of the kingdom. She has also traveled to various states doing Kingdom building and traveled to Sierra Leone Africa on a seven-day Crusade.

She is a graduate of Wilmington University with a Bachelor of Science in Early Childhood Education.

For the past 13 years, she has run a family childcare center out of her home and is a certified Child Advocate and Early Childhood Special Education in the state of Delaware. Additionally, she worked in the Human Service field for 20 years, working with both children and adults with special needs. Darlinda enjoys being creative and has a passion for sewing and singing. She also has her own catering business coordinating weddings and social affairs. She is a Children's Book writer. She and her husband Claret reside in Delaware and have five children and four grandchildren.

BIOGRAPHICAL SKETCH

Spiritual shepherd, ministerial and business visionary, Bishop Reuben Timothy Jones, Jr., was born and reared in Philadelphia, Pennsylvania and received his education in the Philadelphia Public School System. He is the eldest of two children born to the late Bishop and Mother R.T. Jones, Sr., founders of Christian Tabernacle Friendly Community COGIC of Philadelphia, PA. In 2004, the Lord led Bishop Jones to rename the church to Jones Memorial Friendly Community COGIC in memory of the late founders.

Being obedient to the voice of God, Bishop Jones acknowledged his call to ministry and began preaching in 1959. The late Bishop O. T. Jones, Sr., ordained him in September of 1962. In 1973, Pastor Jones founded Christian Tabernacle Friendly Community COGIC in Chester, PA, where he served as Pastor for nine years. In 1990, he became Pastor of Christian Tabernacle COGIC in Philadelphia, PA after the untimely death of his father,

Bishop R. T. Jones, Sr.

He attended Cheyney University and the Reformed Episcopal Seminary. In 1996, he was honored by the Martha's Vineyard Seminary with a Doctor of Divinity Degree. Also in 1996, he was presented the "Speak up for America" Award. As a man of vision, Bishop Jones is revered by many as a dynamic man of wisdom, leadership, integrity, and compassion. In addition to his commitment to Christian Tabernacle as senior pastor, Bishop Jones has served his community in numerous roles that include service to Temple University Health Services, and Chairman on the Community Planning Committee. He also serves in various positions on an array of boards including: the Opportunities Industrialization Center (OIC), founded in 1964 by the late Rev. Leon Sullivan and others. His secular work includes employment with the Philadelphia Police Department and Philadelphia Housing Authority. He also served his country in the United States Marine Corp.

His consecration to the Bishopric occurred in 1975 in the Church of God in Christ, International, Inc., by the late Bishop I.L. Jefferson. In 1976, he was appointed as Superintendent of the Southeastern Jurisdiction of PA.

In 2012, he has become the Superintendent of the Unity District of the PA Koinonia Jurisdiction under Bishop Ernest C. Morris. He is the Father of six children and the proud grandfather of twelve. He is presently married to his lovely wife, Anita.

Bishop Jones' ministry delivers a message of hope and love in the midst of a dying world. His messages teach that we have a hope in Christ Jesus who is the "author and finisher of our faith." His charismatic style, scriptural approach, and anointed ministry of song are inclusive of his methods to stimulate the hearts and minds of those searching for their "way out." Through his anointed messages, yokes have been broken by penetrating stony hearts and convincing the ungodly that God is love, and he is able to save anybody.

He is recognized as one of the great preachers of this generation with a message that ministers to the whole person, and he brings together people of various backgrounds, age groups, and ethnicities. Bishop Jones devotes his life to preaching the gospel of Jesus Christ.

He faithfully seeks to be led by the anointing of the Holy Ghost, through Bishop Jones is abundantly blessed by the Lord and is very grateful for God's favor on his life.

He is a very kind, generous, and down-to-earth gentleman who remains a most humble servant of the Lord. He is a warm, considerate humanitarian who cares about his neighbor showing the love of Jesus Christ to his fellow man. He can be seen and heard every Sunday morning in worship at Jones Memorial COGIC.

In 2017, Bishop Jones retired from the pastorate. He understood that there needed to be a change in the season of his life. He presently serves in the Koinonia Jurisdiction of PA as an administrative assistant to Bishop EC Morris, prelate of the Jurisdiction. Bishop Jones has ministered in Africa and Korea. He has traveled to Argentina, Brazil, Rome, and England. Even after 61 years in ministry, he is yet ready, willing, and able to serve this present age, his calling to fulfill, with all his power engaged to do the Master's will.

WE THANK YOU!

Made in the USA
Middletown, DE
25 March 2024

51849630R00066